Love Letters From Your Body

SABINA SINGWELL, PHD

B CRAFT PRODUCTIONS

Contents

Introduction	1
Day 1	4
Your body is a chamber of sensation	
Day 2	6
Chasing perfection	
Day 3	8
You are worth fighting for	
Day 4	10
I'll do me, you do you	
Day 5	11
Making space for self-soothing	
Day 6	13
You are deserving of love	
Day 7	15
Your shame is optional	
Day 8	17
You are a piece of the universe	
Day 9	19
Our belly is awesome	
Day 10	21
Feel it all	
Day 11	23
The wonder of us	
Day 12	26
So what?	
Day 13	29
An intentional zigzag	
Day 14	32
In the flow of life	
Day 15	34
Pleasure	
Day 16	36
Releasing emotion	

Day 17 *Your body is your life*	38
Day 18 *Writing to your body*	40
Day 19 *Chasing peace*	42
Day 20 *Check me out*	44
Day 21 *Everything changes*	46
Day 22 *Food is not (meant to be) a threat*	48
Day 23 *Living in allowance*	50
Day 24 *Let them judge you. You are Divine*	52
Day 25 *You are enough*	54
Day 26 *Human on a floating rock*	55
Day 27 *You are a delightful corgi (or poodle or pug...)*	57
Day 28 *Having a human experience*	60
Day 29 *Already perfect*	63
Day 30 *Which side are you on?*	65
Day 31 *A love letter from the author*	68

Introduction

Hello Darling,

In the past few years, a new expectation has arisen for women. It's no longer enough for us to contort ourselves to meet an impossible beauty standard; now we have to "love the skin we're in" while simultaneously being told to buy multiple products to modify that very skin.

Body positivity has gone from a political movement to a hollowed-out slogan used to sell jeans, another tick box on the checklist of gendered requirements for our lives. We're now expected to happily perform "body love," and if we don't "embrace our curves," we feel guilty for our supposed failure.

This doesn't mean that the whole effort to divest ourselves from body hatred isn't a worthwhile effort. Once we put aside the *expectation* that we should be in a constant state of rapture about how beautiful our bodies are, we can make room for more complicated feelings.

The reality is that befriending your body in a culture that taught you to mistrust, judge and criticize it can be massively life-enhancing. But connecting meaningfully to our bodies takes so much more than just throwing body-positive affirmations at it.

So what if, instead of trying to convince ourselves that our bodies are worthy of love, we connect to that sense of love through the body itself? What if a feeling of love for our bodies didn't come from our brains, but vice versa? What if your body sent love to your mind instead of the other way around?

Tuning in to an embodied sense of love can be a powerful tool in the toolbox for healing body image. I know, because I'm a writer and body-image coach who teaches women and non-binary folks about how to divest from a culture of body hatred and invest in a sensation of body *righteousness*.

This practice of conjuring a sense of love FOR the body by connecting TO the sensation of love in the body is one of my favourite things to teach.

In fact, that's the origin of this little booklet of love letters from the body.

Written as a series of emails to be read each day in December 2022, these letters provide a month's worth of guidance back to the sensation of love in your body. Each time you connect to that sensation, it builds up a new pathway that can lead you to feel more grounded and at ease in your body.

Use these letters in the way that best suits you. You can:

- read just one letter per day for 31 days (and start all over again!).
- print it out (if you bought the digital download from my store), read the whole thing, mark it up with your own notes, and come back to it when you need it.

- add it to any list of resources or tools in the body-image toolkit you use when you need a pick-me-up.

Regardless of how you use them, just remember that, like your own heart, these letters are always here for you when you need them.

The best part is, if you want more love letters, I've got you covered. Every Thursday, I send a love letter from your body to folks who subscribe to my Substack newsletter. Head to my website SchoolOfBitchcraft.com and sign up to keep receiving your love-letter goodness.

Xoxoxo,
Sabina Singwell

Day 1

YOUR BODY IS A CHAMBER OF SENSATION

Hello, Darling,

How do you know, at any given moment, what emotion you are feeling?

You physically feel it in your body.

After all, that's what an emotion is: a felt sense inside of you that provides you with information.

Regardless of what label we put on those feelings, when the blood is pounding in your ears, hair is standing up on your arms, or your jaw is clenching up, those are your emotions speaking to you through your body.

Living in this body is your chance to experience the full buffet of human emotions. And what a buffet there is! You've got stuff like:

- hope, anticipation, fulfillment, satisfaction;
- joy, happiness, contentment;
- connection, desire, love;

- melancholy, longing, loneliness, emptiness;
- sadness, grief, loss;
- anger, resentment, envy, fear.

And the thing is... you can only experience these emotions inside your body. Yes, this animated meatsack is the ONLY PLACE IN THE WORLD where you will EVER feel these feelings! Your body, this body, is a chamber for resonance and sensation that flows in and out in an endless, vibrant spiral.

So for today, here is what your body wants you to know:

Today and every day, rushes of feeling will course through us. Each feeling is an opportunity for you to sense into the goldmine of information I'm conveying to you. You may feel our stomach clench with dread or ache with laughter, our chest open with joy and close with defensiveness, our toes grip with anxiety or wiggle with glee.

All I want for you is to feel it all. At every moment, I am here for you, always available for you to experience every sensation. In moments when it's safe and reasonable, I absolutely relish you tuning in to me. In return, I will remind you that you are simply alive.

Love,
Your Body

Day 2

CHASING PERFECTION

Hello, Darling,

Perfection is not a state for a future self to achieve, but for the present self to behold. "Perfect" is already here.

It's in each breath we draw, each moment of connection with someone we love, each beam of sunlight that travels *93 million miles* through outer space to hit our skin.

But.

Some people really, really bristle at the idea that their body is already perfect just as it is. *Clearly that is not the case*, they say, as they look down and gesture at it. Maybe they have a disability, or an illness, or their body doesn't meet the prevailing beauty standard. *There is suffering here*, they say. *This body needs to change in order to alleviate the suffering.*

I never want to deny people's experiences of their lives and their bodies. But I also know this:

Alleviating the suffering you experience in your body begins with changing the story you tell yourself about it.

Opening yourself up to the possibility that we've got a both/and situation here — that there is perfection *and* suffering in this here body right now — can be the beginning of changing that painful story.

So this is what your body wants you to know today:

I know I sometimes disappoint you. I know I frustrate you. I know there are things you'd like to pluck right out of me, parts of me you'd like to erase. I get that and accept that.

What I want YOU to get and accept in return is that your survival is the only thing I care about. I am definitely fallible (I mean, I am a delicate animated meatsack... fallible is kinda built right in) and sometimes some dumbass cells go off and do dumbass shit.

But believe me, I am keeping you alive today by running so many intricate, finely balanced processes and systems that even the best doctors and scientists in the world still don't understand it all. This work of keeping you breathing and eating and pooping and moving and laughing and thinking and loving is the work of my very life and I love doing it.

And you don't even need to love me back in order for me to do it. It's already perfect.

Love,
Your Body

Day 3

YOU ARE WORTH FIGHTING FOR

Hello, Darling,

You know how yesterday I said that alleviating the suffering you experience over your body has to begin with changing your story about it?

That is true, and it's also only half-true.

The other half of the truth about your suffering is that it is shared with countless others.

So many of us live in a silent community of people whose bodies result in their exclusion from certain places or people or jobs.

Sometimes this is simply a feeling to manage, but sometimes it's a reality. Ableism really does present access barriers for people with disabilities. Racism, sexism, homophobia, transphobia, fatphobia, poverty and other forms of oppression really do create and perpetuate conditions of un-safety and discrimination. They have the power, quite simply, to crush us.

The solution is not to "feel good" your way out of these oppressive conditions (if these are the conditions you are facing or that you care about).

However, viewing yourself and your body as something and somebody worth fighting for can *fuel* the social change you believe in.

It doesn't matter whether you want to fight forms of oppression through activism, education, policy tools, legal reform, or wholesale chucking the system out entirely. Shifting the story you have been telling yourself for years (or decades) about how bad and broken and inadequate your body is, is key to advancing the change you want to see in the world.

That's why Audre Lorde said that self-care was a revolutionary act. She wasn't talking about taking bubble baths (not that there is anything wrong with bubble baths). She meant that *caring about your very being in a world that may not care that much about you is bold and brave as fuck.*

Bottom line: in order to fight oppression, it very much helps to view yourself and your body as something worth fighting for.

So today, your body says:

My skin colour, my ethnicity, my dis/abiliy, my gender, the size of my thighs, who we love — these are precious aspects of my being and the being of other bodies that look like me and love like me. I — we — are worth fighting for.

Love,
Your Body

Day 4

I'LL DO ME, YOU DO YOU

Hello, Darling,

It's me, your body. I'm so glad to be here, today, pulsing and beating and alive.

I know sometimes you can be a bit mean to me, especially when you're feeling anxious about something. I know a lot of the time it doesn't even have anything to do with me. You'll be feeling worried about something at work or in a relationship or whatever and – BLAMMO! – you suddenly start taking it out on me. I understand.

I'm just going to keep doing me, though, just living our life for us. And I'm going to keep doing it because I really love you.

I'll talk to you later today, ok? I'll tell you when I'm hungry, when I need to pee, when I need to sneeze, if I need a stretch or a cuddle or a nap. Because we are great partners like that.

Love,
Your Body

Day 5

MAKING SPACE FOR SELF-SOOTHING

Dearest Darling,

What do days off mean for you? Sleeping in? Batch cooking for the week? Getting out for a long run? Flopping down for a Netflix marathon? Simply showering?

All sound great and all are morally neutral. You are the boss of you, and only YOU can say what YOU need to put gas in YOUR tank for the coming week.

Other people's lists of self-care methods are nice and all, but may not resonate with you and the season you're in right now. Green juice and yoga work for some, but are not, in fact, the height of self-care for every person on the planet.

Even your own self-care list is going to change and evolve over time, based on current demands, the phase of life you're in, and your ever-changing physical, emotional, intellectual, financial, spiritual and community needs. It even depends on the weather!

Taking care of you to the best of your ability doesn't always come easy. The difficulty is due largely to three factors:

- the multiple demands on our time;
- our own internal dialogue about what kind of respite we're entitled to; and
- the very systems from which we are seeking to recuperate never really stop bearing down on us.

That's why whatever you do to sustain yourself, let it be something that responds to who you are and what you need *today*.

And so, today your body says,

My nervous system knows when you're play-acting at self-care, and when you're truly soothing us. Sometimes what we need is sleep, sometimes it's a slow walk, sometimes it's jumping and dancing around; sometimes those things are the LAST thing we need and actually make it harder for us.

The most important thing is a) to tune in to me and b) make space for what you hear the answer to be.

Love,
Your Body

Day 6

YOU ARE DESERVING OF LOVE

Hello, Darling,

You came into this world as a gorgeous being deserving of love.

And guess what?

That is what you still are: **a gorgeous being deserving of love**.

Nothing about your body or your size or skin colour or gender or disability changes that.

Nothing.

The un-loving things you've learned to internalize about your body to this point are just that: learned. They're not innate.

Love, relentless love, is the way to un-learning your supposed brokenness, and the path back to the knowing of your own wholeness.

So today your body says:

Love me not in defiance of the society that taught you to hate me.
Love me simply so that you can return home to me.

Love,
Your Body

Day 7

YOUR SHAME IS OPTIONAL

H ello, Darling,

Today, your body has some thoughts on food.

Listen. You know how sometimes we eat some things and then we feel a bit yucky after? That yucky feeling is me looking out for you. That's just me saying, "Whoa, slow down, partner! I need a sec to digest this."

When I send you that signal, it's not a cue for you to start shaming yourself. That's just me sending you a note saying, "please pause, I'm sorting out the digestion situation rn. Get back to me shortly."

But you gotta know, when you start berating yourself and being all "I can't believe I ate [all] that!" it actually makes it so much harder for me to do my job. I get all constricted, and there is also research that shows that I absorb fewer nutrients when you get all wound up like that.

*Sometimes your mean thoughts about me can even **give** you the gastro-intestinal symptoms that you think you got from the food* *you ate. It's not (always) the food! It's the anxiety and the mean-ass thoughts, babe!*

All I'm saying is this: I have an incredible capacity to handle ALL KINDS of curve balls you throw at me. Sometimes you don't let me have enough sleep, and I just deal with that, right? Sometimes you don't water me enough, but I do my best to squeeze out every drop before your pee becomes an impressive yellow, no?

I am so fuckin' resilient, and I just want you to keep that in mind the next time you go hard at the buffet table, ok? When I give you the signal, just give me some water and a little lie-down and we will be all right. Your shame is optional.

Love,
Your Body

Day 8

YOU ARE A PIECE OF THE UNIVERSE

Hello, Darling,

Do you remember when the images from the James Webb Telescope were publicly released, back in the summer of 2022? The absolutely striking images showed glowing cloudscapes, sparkling star fields, nebulae comprised of ridges, peaks and valleys that looked so akin to earth's mountain ranges. Breathtakingly spectacular, it felt astonishing to look at these images and consider the literally awesome vast expanse of the universe.

And do you want to know something really cool?

To paraphrase Geneen Roth, *your body is the piece of the universe you have been given*. Your body, this body! Is part of THAT PHENOMENAL UNIVERSE! You are a part of each other, brilliantly and profoundly interconnected. WOW!

So your love note from your body today is:

This body you inhabit is as worthy of awe and marvel as the rest of the universe.

Love,
Your Body

Day 9

OUR BELLY IS AWESOME

H ello, Darling,

I have an invitation for you.

Could you, for ten or twenty seconds, lightly and lovingly put your hand on your own stomach, if you are physically and emotionally able?

Not to pinch your flesh or poke to see if your abs are there or admire it or bemoan it in a mirror.

But to just lovingly let your hand come to rest on your vulnerable, vulnerable belly.

Can you take five seconds right now to just inhabit it? Feel it? Be there with it and for it?

Mmmm. Yes. Belly! That's your belly. And I don't care how round or hard or soft or convex or concave it is. It's your belly and it is lovely and loveable. It really is.

Today, your belly is just going to do what it's supposed to do: process your food into energy units and poop out the rest.

(Of course, it does so many other things, too, things that are so cool we barely know about or understand them! Like doing smart, funky shit with your microbiome, and sending information up and down your Vagus nerve!)

So just take this as a reminder that belly is fucking cool. It does all that stuff without you even knowing anything about it. Do YOU know how to take food, turn it into energy units and turn the waste into poop? No, you do not, because you are not and have never been in charge of doing that. Why? BECAUSE YOUR BELLY IS THE BABE WHO DOES THAT FOR YOU, NO QUESTIONS ASKED.

(OK, fine, sometimes she asks questions, like why you had to have three glasses of wine on an empty stomach, but even then, when she asks you why you did that, she's doing her job — marvellously!).

So if you can, find a moment or two today when you can put your hand on your belly, remember all her hard work, and give her a little "thank you" for doing what she does for you.

Because today your body wants you to know:

Our belly is awesome, babe.

Love,
Your Body

Day 10

FEEL IT ALL

Hello, Darling,

Here is a top tip on dealing with big feelings from actor Lili Reinhart, pulled from a podcast interview with host Jay Shetty:

"If I started out as this celestial being — just energy — and the universe or God or whomever said, 'Hey, do you want to go to Earth for an incredibly short amount of time — like a blip — and experience every emotion you could possibly feel as a human...

You get to have all these experiences: love, heartache, anxiety, joy, euphoria, whatever. All of it. Do you want to do that?'

'Yeah, I do.'

And so, when I am feeling these intense feelings, it's sort of like a reality check to step outside and say, 'Although this is a very uncomfortable, painful feeling, it's quite beautiful that I have the capacity to experience it.'

That is something that I use to ground myself when I am stuck in a feeling of darkness."

So today, your body reminds you:

We have the marvellous capacity to feel it all, for just a brief blip of time, and that is beautiful.

Love,
Your Body

Day 11

THE WONDER OF US

Hello, Darling,

Yesterday, I invited you to rest your hand on your stomach, to just tune in to her and sense her and maybe thank her for all her hard work.

Today, I have an invitation to go even deeper into that sensing. It's an opportunity to tune in to the very presence of your own body. It's an embodiment exercise you can learn to do and pull out anytime, anywhere. No yoga mat required.

This is inspired by the late Deneen Fendig, and her appearance on her son Duncan Trussell's podcast.

This tool offers a subtle but profound shift in your consciousness as a result of tuning in to your body's presence. It is a wonderful practice that short-circuits your brain's insistence on narrating to you about your body's existence and tunes you right into the amazingness of your own being.

In doing so, you can better understand your body as so much more than an ornament or instrument. Instead, it is a being absolutely thrumming with live, crackling energy.

You don't need to be in any particular physical place or posture, but you do need to be able to safely tune in to yourself and kinda let the outside world go for a few minutes. You could be standing on a crowded bus, sitting at your cubicle at work, watching TV or even cooking dinner (you might want to put down any sharp knives and switch off anything that's on the stove, though).

To begin, let's start with focusing on your right hand (if you have a disability and don't have the use of your right hand, switch to another available appendage).

Relax the hand completely. Now tune in to it. You don't need to look at it or touch it unless that helps to tune in to it. But what you actually want to do here is sense what your hand feels like *from the inside*.

Listen to it with the same ears you would use to listen to the wind rustling in the trees. It might take you a few moments to fully tune in, but the sensation is obvious once you do.

What does it feel like? Warm? Sort of buzzy? Alive? Kinda…throbby?

Whatever it feels like is perfectly wonderful, just as it is. All you're doing here is just noticing, without judging or labelling. Take as much time as you want just feeling the sensation of your hand.

When you're ready, see if you are able to move that feeling up from your hand to your arm. Then try it with your left hand and left arm. Move the feeling through your shoulders and chest and belly, and then move down your legs to your toes.

This is your body! It is here just for you! It is YOUR unique vessel in the world and it is FABULOUS.

If you want to get super advanced, once you've dropped into that full-body attunement, you can let your gaze land on the space in front of you and around you. Here you can sense the presence of you as a being in relation to other beings or objects in the world.

Isn't that so cool?

So today, your body says,

I am always available for you to experience the wonder of me, and the wonder of the world around you.

Love,
Your Body

Day 12

SO WHAT?

Hello, Darling,

Here is a little game you can play when you find your brain messing with you. Let's say you have a moment of anxiety that you decide to take out on your body, or you catch a glimpse of your reflection in the mirror and the decades-old recording about how horrible your body is starts up.

This game is called "so what?" and it is exactly what it sounds like. For every freaked-out thought your dumbass brain sends you about how hideous you are, you just come right back at it and ask, "so what?"

For me, this game can look like this:

> Brain: "Man, WTH, you look like SHIT right now."

> Me: So what?

> Brain: Well, you look so OLD. How can you walk around in public looking so OLD?

Me: OK, I look old. So what?

Brain: Well… you're not supposed to.

Me: OK, but I do. So what?

Brain: Um… well, people might ignore you. They might discriminate against you. WHAT ABOUT AGEISM?!

Me: Yes, ageism is a real bitch. I don't think that being mean to myself about it is going to make it easier for me to deal with it, though.

Brain: Yeah, but you look, like, UGLY.

Me: OK. So what?

Brain: Well… nobody is going to love you!!!

Me: I have plenty of evidence that I am loved. And also, I love me.

Brain: "eah, but THAT'S NOT GOOD ENOUGH!!!

Me: Why?

Brain: Um… because you're supposed to be loved by EVERYBODY!

Me: I'm not loved by everybody and I never will be. Plenty of people dislike me and some may even hate me. So what?

Brain: Well… that's uncomfortable!!!

Me: So what? We've been handling discomfort all our life.

Brain: I give up.

And then I get on with my day.

You can try this with your own brain by volleying back "why?" or "so what?" each time the part of you that wants to sabotage or keep you small starts piping up. Sometimes this practice squashes the mean thought instantly. Sometimes it begins a long round of volleys back and forth between your most scared, constricted self and your most present, grounded self. It can be a fruitful way to sense into the part of you that knows she can handle whatever life throws at her.

So today, your body lovingly says to you:

So what? We've got this.

Love,
Your Body

Day 13

AN INTENTIONAL ZIGZAG

Hello, Darling,

Sometimes your body sends you signals that you don't actually want to sense, or that are difficult to discern. This sometimes happens during moments where the idea of tuning into the body feels inconvenient or annoying. This, in turn, can produce tension in us, so what we often end up doing is just picking up our phones to distract ourselves.

Now, not every spare moment of your day has to be spent in a yoga pose being perfectly tuned in to what your body is trying to whisper to you. That is not only incredibly tedious, it's that perfectionist posing that so-called "wellness" culture encourages us to do – but which doesn't ultimately serve anyone except companies selling yoga mats.

The middle ground between pretending to be a perfectly attuned yogi and being glued to our pocket computers can be found in some of the quotidian pleasures of life. Spending just two minutes having a little intentional experience can help shift things inside you.

Here are a few ideas for these two-minute experiences.

Things You Can Do to Just Feel Something Instead of Scrolling Through the Same Three Social Media Apps You Always Do

- Write a list of the very predictable things this list would typically include (e.g. go for a walk, do some deep breathing, yoga), and then scratch off the list anything that just doesn't sound suitable to you at all right now.
- Read a poem, preferably by Ross Gay (you can look him up on the Poetry Foundation website, poetryfoundation.org.)
- Flip through the oldest cookbook you have on your shelf and get lost in the memories.
- Focus your attention on your hands and rediscover what it feels like to have them (see Day 11).
- Lie down on the floor.
- Look around at your surroundings and really, really see them (while still lying on the floor or not).
- Marvel at the many different directions your arm can move.
- Put some water in a wine glass and drag your wet finger along its edge to hear what tone it makes.
- Unclench your jaw.
- Pretend. Pretend anything. Just play pretend.

What else might you do that you would put on a list just for YOU?

Today, your body says,

Sometimes the best way of approaching me is by zigging and zagging, instead of just getting down to business. Play around, and you'll likely generate a bunch more ideas you can put on this list.

Love,
Your Body

Day 14

IN THE FLOW OF LIFE

H ello, Darling,

What is a body for?

What is YOUR body for?

As I contemplated this question, I wrote out this silly little list-poem:

Kissing / eating / hugging / dancing /

singing / fucking / chewing / laughing /

protesting / fighting / pushing / pulling

writing / reading / cooking / looking

fawning / freezing / overheating /

holding / walking / screaming / breathing /

observing / talking / kneading / chopping /

starting / stopping / popcorn popping /

running / shrieking / thinking / drinking

squatting / freezing / squeezing / freaking

Maybe some of these apply to you, too, or maybe you'd come up with entirely different verbs. The list could be endless!

That's because the experiences your body offers you each day is endless. Even if you have chronic pain, a disability, or an elbow that gets stiff when it rains. Possibility is always right here with us.

So today, your body wants to tell you:

We're not stuck. We are never stuck. Being stuck for us is as possible as the ocean being stuck. We are always, always in motion, and always in the middle of the flow of life.

Love,
Your Body

PLEASURE

Hello, Darling,

Have you perused the sex-toy market lately?

These days, there are toys that suck and blow, toys with all kinds of textures and curves and angles, toys that sync to your phone and pulse and do your taxes.

Back in my day, all we had was an on and off switch!

So if you:

a) don't have a special toy you can use just for your body's sexual pleasure, with or without a partner, or

b) haven't explored the array of available toy options since the Clinton administration,

then your task for today is to consider whether your body might like one. And if she does, go ahead and ask her what might most interest her.

Making space for sexual pleasure, among all the other pleasures of life, is a wonderful way to experience the wonder of being alive and the wonder of being YOU. (Unless you are asexual, in which case, please disregard this love letter! I see you and validate you!)

So today, your body says:

Let's get it on.

Love,
Your Body

Day 16

RELEASING EMOTION

Heya, my Darling,

Sometimes we all just need to have a good cry. (Personally, when I feel that way, I turn on *Moana*. It does the trick every time.)

But depending on what's happening for you, sometimes other forms of energy release will do, too.

Have you ever tried jumping or shaking as a way to get out intense feelings of nervousness or even anger? It can initially feel kind of embarrassing, but it actually does wonders for the nervous system.

How about dancing or some good, old-fashioned flailing?

Sometimes deep stretching can do the job, especially if that coincides with some giant jaw stretches, perhaps accompanied by a wee bit of growling or screaming.

What other things can you think of?

Today, your body says:

Remember that I feel all your feelings. So listening intently when I release intense emotions can feel fantastic, especially during those times when exercise or getting outside feels impossible to do.

Love,
Your Body

YOUR BODY IS YOUR LIFE

Hello, Darling,

Today I have a really useful exercise for you, something that you can come back to over and over, especially in moments when you find yourself being really mean to yourself.

This exercise begins with understanding that your body is your very life. She is your best friend. She looks out for you in a multitude of ways. Your survival is her No. 1 priority. You wouldn't be able to live your life if it weren't for her.

What happens inside your body when you start thinking about her in this way? Where does softness come in? Where does tension loosen?

How do your thoughts about her change? Can you sense compassion towards her? Can you sense gratitude or love towards her?

As you begin to consider that this human being right here is your best friend in the whole wide world, consider giving her a name. Consider how you may want to start addressing her. After all, would you ever talk to your best friend the way that you've been talking to yourself up to now?

She's your best friend, and deserves to be spoken to with gentleness and reverence. She is the Michelle to your Barack, the Thelma to your Louise, the Matt Damon to your Ben Affleck. She's got your back. Do you have hers?

Today, your body says to you:

Oh, bestie. We are a team, you and I. I would love to receive the kindness that you offer to other friends, but I know that that may feel difficult, especially at first.

You may believe that the best way for me to do what you want is to criticize and shame me, so speaking to me warmly may feel scary. You may fear you're letting me off the hook.

But believe me, bestie, the better our relationship is, the better your life is.

Love,
Your Body

Day 18

WRITING TO YOUR BODY

Hello, Darling,

If you've enjoyed reading these love letters from your body, what do you think about *writing* a love letter to your body? Are you ready for something like this, or does it feel like a bridge too far?

If you think you could do it, consider what you might want to say in this love letter.

Maybe you'd want to write about all that she's done for you, including:

- The distances her feet have walked for you and the hours she's danced for you;
- The hungers she's inspired in you and the energy output she has produced for you;
- The songs her vocal chords have sung, the "I love you"s she's uttered, the belly laughs she's ripped forth from you;
- The delicious orgasms she's coursed through you;

- The punches she's thrown defending you and the words she's screamed on your behalf;
- The food her hands have prepared, the touches she has offered, the middle fingers her hands have extended.

Just because it's a love letter doesn't mean it has to be toxically positive. Would you want to have a paragraph about the ways she's let you down or made you angry? If you do, that could open up space for her to whisper back with some knowledge or inner knowing about those things.

See how all this feels. It can be a one-time exercise or an ongoing thing (remember to give her a name so you can really address her properly!). It could lead to an entirely different kind of unfolding conversation than you've ever had with your body.

So today your body says,

I'm ready to hear a new kind of message from you.

Love,
Your Body

Day 19

CHASING PEACE

Hello, Darling,

So much of what we want in life is actually about what we imagine we'll have once we get it. And a lot of what we ultimately want is actually peace.

It's kind of amazing how easy *and* how difficult it is to cultivate peace, and how little we are taught about accessing it. We tell ourselves lots of stories about what will lead to peace, like:

- Once I lose weight, then I will be able to relax and know peace.
- Once I get this new outfit, my wardrobe will be complete and I will feel peaceful.
- Once I get this new job/opportunity/grant/book, I will be happy.
- Once I earn this person's love/respect/attention, I will be happy and at peace.

And then remarkably... peace STILL doesn't arrive, even after those things do!

Note: If you don't have the basic essentials of life — clothing, food, water, and a safe place to live — then, in my opinion, you really can't know peace. Your survival instinct will want those things for you so badly that it won't let you know peace until you secure them. This category of things — those that we need as humans to stay alive — is different from the examples of wanting or desire that I'm talking about.

Beyond these things our organism needs, though? Peace can be found within ourselves. As the Buddhist leader Thich Nhat Han once wrote, peace is every step.

Connecting to peace in the present moment is just one of those many exercises that *defines* a practice: something you do over and over and over again, not a destination you ever get to.

That's certainly how it is with reaching a détente with your body, even if it's a temporary one that lasts a few minutes or hours. You remember and forget that you can touch a peace within yourself that is always there, waiting for you. Once or twice or dozens of times a day, you come back to that deep knowing that body hatred is optional. In that split second, you can feel your body ease a bit, almost internally smile, and say:

Yeah, we're good. We're safe. We're gonna be ok.

Love,
Your Body

Day 20

CHECK ME OUT

Wow, my Darling,

Look at you. What a beauty you are!

You are a vision of ferocity and grace. You are a capable, compassionate, clear-hearted wonder. You are a magnet for abundance. You offer good vibes and great times. You love ardently, give with generosity, and fight skillfully.

You, in short, kick ASS.

And look at that bod! Doing the thing and making it happen! Taking in energy and expending it with thought and care! Cells are multiplying, neurons are firing, white blood cells are sentries at the gate! Limbs are limbing, eyeballs are seriously doing their best, and the feet, oh, the FEET! For those of us able to walk, we will never, EVER be able to repay what the feet offer us every damn day. For those of us who are wheelchair or assistive-device users, CHECK OUT THOSE ADORABLE TOES!

Daaaaamn! What an A+ body you got going on there. 10/10, no notes. I hope today you are feeling as fine as that body, you sweet thing.

Today, your body says,

Check me out, world! I am ALIVE!

*Love,
Your Body*

Day 21

EVERYTHING CHANGES

Hello, Darling,

Everything changes.

Indeed, everything *must* change, as Nina Simone sang.

This includes our bodies.

It's ok that you don't have the body you had ten or twenty or thirty years ago because you're not the same person you were back then. In fact, it's entirely *desirable* that you don't have the same body. This is the body that has learned so much, become so natural at doing new things that used to be so challenging. This body has *grown*, physically and mentally.

We generally try to hide away from this fact, but right now, we are living smack dab in the midst of the circle of life. The changes to our body reflect that. It's truly how things are and should be, as painful and sad and grief-laden as that can be. What a privilege that we've been able to see and do and hear and smell and touch things this year that so many people who never got to our age didn't (not to mention the previous you, who hadn't reached this point yet, either).

The you who lit birthday candles last year is not the you who lights them this year. The you who sings and eats and talks and thinks today is not the you who did those things last year or five years ago or twenty years ago. And isn't that splendid?

Today, your body says,

The breath in our lungs is just as it should be. The wrinkles and scars and curves and angles are just as they should be. The aches and pains remind us of our humanity, which is just as it should be.

Blessed be,
Your Body

Day 22

FOOD IS NOT (MEANT TO BE) A THREAT

Hiya, Darling,

Sometimes when we sit down in front of a plate of food, or even just contemplate eating, we feel a tightness inside. We might feel a pang of worry or guilt due to what we've heard about the dangers or health impact of this or that food.

The reality is, if it's edible and you're not allergic to it, no single meal is going to cause you harm.

When we "misidentify food as a threat," (as Gwyneth Olwyn puts it), we are on a particular plane of suffering that can make life really hellish. If you and your body are having a screaming match because your body really wants a slice of bread and your diet brain thinks that you "shouldn't" because of what it will do to you… well, there's nothing health-promoting about that.

If this is your experience, learning that there is nothing on our plates to guard against can be enormously difficult. But without learning it, we are doomed to live a life in opposition and struggle with eating.

Just know that you don't have to live your life like that forever. There are lots of resources out there to help you deal with this particular form of hell.

Your body wants you to know:

It is possible for us to live in harmonious alignment. We don't have to live our life screaming at each other.

Love,
Your Body

Day 23

LIVING IN ALLOWANCE

Hello, Darling,

The reason why you're allowed to eat is because it is a requirement for your ongoing existence. You are allowed to exist.

There is nothing about you that is so wrong that you are not allowed to exist. There is nothing about you that is so wrong that you are not allowed to eat.

But the *belief* that there is something wrong is what gets you tangled up in knots at the dinner table.

Those knots can feel especially tight if you are sitting at that dinner table with the very people who taught you that belief.

If you will be spending time with people who taught you your body is incorrect, I am so very, very, very sorry. I would like to send you the biggest, longest hug.

But because I can't do that, I am tasking *you* with doing that. Wrap the saddest, most hurt, most dejected part of you in the warmest embrace, the one you reserve for those you love most.

Remind yourself: you've got your own back.

Remind yourself that your body is not a "situation" to be "managed."

Remind yourself that your body is simply the sparkling, unique, temporarily animated human flesh that is *you*.

You get to exist in the body that *you* inhabit today.

And *you* are allowed and encouraged to care for this body today by eating the food that you want.

Today, your body says,

I am the unrepeatable being of energy that is you.

Love,
Your Body

Day 24

LET THEM JUDGE YOU. YOU ARE DIVINE

Hello, Darling,

No matter how confident we are, we all have moments when we feel nervous about people judging our body or our appearance.

Here is the thing to keep in mind in those moments.

There are people in the world who soften inside when they see you. You come through the doorway and they instantly smile. They maybe feel a little giggly and a lot safe with you. They take you in and their nervous systems ease out a little bit. Even the excitement and joy they feel at seeing you is a type of softening. Even the spark they feel is one of comfort. They feel it in their bellies, or up in their chest, or right in the solar plexus.

Then there are other people who… meh, not so much.

And it's the same way for you, too, right? People who make you feel connected and others who kinda make you go, "alllll righty, then!"

The ones in whom you spark joy don't really give a shit about what you look like. They already know you're gorgeous. They don't have any agenda for you, except for you to be happy and alive and as fully your awesome self as possible. They are the only people you really have to care about, and what you DON'T have to care about with them is what they think of your face, your neck, your waistline or your booty.

Then there are the rest, the "meh" folks, the ones you smile and nod for. Maybe they love you, maybe you love them, maybe not, but either way, meh — their opinion doesn't really matter very much.

And it doesn't really matter if this person is your mother or an old friend or a distant cousin. They are going to think whatever they're going to think, so you know what? **LET THEM**. Just let them. Feel the freedom of letting go of trying to control other people's thoughts and actions. It's not worth it, and it never works anyway!

So today, your body says,

Listen, we can face anybody as long as we work together, okay? You decide if you want to bring the main-character energy or not, and I'll make sure it sparkles forth from you. I'll keep the nervous system calm and keep you breathing, and you make choices like packing up and going home if you feel my heart start racing. Be sure to keep up my energy stores by feeding me, and let's stay at ease by chatting with someone we can have a laugh with (I'll give us a little chemical release if you're able to do that). And don't forget, babe — we are going to look literally DIVINE to the people who love us the most.

Love,
Your Body

Day 25

YOU ARE ENOUGH

Hello, Darling,

It's your body here, and today I have but a simple reminder:

You are enough.

You are enough.

You are enough.

Regardless of the day you are having today, please take a moment or two and touch the inner peace of knowing your enough-ness today.

Love,
Your Body

Day 26

HUMAN ON A FLOATING ROCK

Hi there, Darling,

We love the illusion that we can control our lives through self-development.

But here's the reality: you don't actually have to change anything about yourself.

You don't have to push yourself, or improve yourself, or "become a better version of you." All of that shit is optional.

You don't even need to try to grow. "Grow" is so often just a euphemism for "reject the person you are now and try to be different."

Do you think a tulip "tries" to grow? No, it just does, because growing is part of its essence. It's honestly no different for you.

You don't have to be anybody else because you — who and how you are today — are enough.

Sure, you have goals and dreams and whatever floats your boat.

Just know that none of that stuff is de facto going to lead to you liking yourself.

If you feel like you have to grow, change, and be "you, only better," in order to like yourself, then your task is not to change but to *attend to the part of you that doesn't like you.*

So get clear on WHY you think you need to change before you jump in.

Today, your body says,

Hey. We're wacky and flawed and yeah, I sometimes don't always do what you want me to. But man! We are also perfect and perfectly formed. We are a human on a floating rock having a human experience. And what could be more beautiful than that?

*Love,
Your body*

Day 27

YOU ARE A DELIGHTFUL CORGI (OR POODLE OR PUG…)

Hello, Darling,

You probably know this already, but it bears repeating: no one engages in body hatred in a vacuum.

It's something that we learn via our messed-up, ableist, diet-addled culture.

If we lived in a world where body acceptance was the norm, diets wouldn't exist. Home scales wouldn't exist. Thighmasters wouldn't exist. And billions of dollars would be diverted elsewhere than into the coffers of corporations that benefit from making people obsess about their bodies.

We would understand that a true diversity of bodies in terms of height, weight, girth, ability, skin tone, texture and colour simply is just a normal human thing and isn't something to resist.

Can you imagine if humans were like dogs, and it was just widely understood that some of us are bulldogs, some of us are greyhounds, some are Chihuahuas, Afghan hounds, poodles, Rottweilers, corgis, huskies, terriers, and Great Danes?

We would never look at our own boobs, booties or bellies (let alone someone else's) and think, FUUUUUUUUUUUUCK.

We'd just be, like, "cool."

But here's the thing — human bodies actually ARE wildly diverse, and they are MEANT to be so. Some of us are just naturally very short! Or tall! Or in between! Similarly, some of us are just naturally very small and light, and some of us are naturally very big and heavy, and most of us fall on a vast range in between.

Even if we all ate the exact same food and moved our bodies in the exact same way, NOTHING about that diversity of bodies would change.

We try to turn our Saint Bernard selves into whippets because we're told that's where the cultural currency is: the promises of happiness, ease, comfort, love, respect and acceptance.

Yet all of the shame, self-punishment, and adherence to the food rules somehow doesn't deliver any of that... because it never could.

Understanding and accepting this requires a massive paradigm shift that takes time. But figuring it out — seeing that the true path to love and peace is not through manipulating your body — is *so worth it*.

So today, your body says:

Is it possible for you to accept me for the lovable [dog you most identify with] that I am? Is it possible to let me play and roam and eat and be just as I am? Is it possible to be loved just as I am?

Love,
Your Body

Day 28

HAVING A HUMAN EXPERIENCE

Hello, Darling,

I've got some good news and some bad news.

The bad news is that as long as you are alive to have human experiences, you'll never be able to get away from the pain of simply being human.

The good news is that as long as you are alive to have human experiences, you get to be alive to have human experiences!!! *Which is kinda mind-blowing!*

Many religions, particularly Buddhism, provide guidance around the difference between human *pain* and human *suffering*.

I dropped out of divinity school, so I can't break it all down for you.

But here is what I do know:

1. As long as you seek relief from your suffering by trying to manipulate your weight, your suffering won't stop.
2. As long as you seek relief from your body hatred from external sources, your suffering won't stop.
3. As long as you use weight loss as a way to finally like yourself, you won't ever like yourself (i.e. your suffering won't stop).

In other words:

1. Your attachment to your body looking a certain way is the thing that is bringing you suffering — not your body itself.
2. Getting ok with who you are and accepting that some people just don't/won't like you are two critical practices to jettisoning avoidable suffering from your life.
3. Trying and trying and trying to get them to like you by losing weight — so that you can finally like yourself — is futile. You'll never, ever get there (not for more than 2 seconds, anyway) because the reality is that *we just can't control what other people think*.

This might feel like a major bummer! But it is, I assure you, good news. There is so much suffering that is in your hands, which means there is *so much you can let go of*.

As scary as it is, there is real freedom in letting go of the idea that you can shame and manipulate your way into liking yourself. There are paths that are far, far richer with goodness and possibility and authenticity.

Maybe what it all boils down to is: *hey, you're ok. You just have to choose to see that.*

Or maybe what your body might say is:

We got this. I'll take care of the energy production, the disease fighting, the gross and fine motor skills, the cell regeneration, the cognition, the hormone sequences and all that stuff — and you just focus on the liking and the loving, ok?

Love,
Your Body

Day 29

ALREADY PERFECT

Dearest Darling,

Here's an idea: consider whether your goals about your body are coming from a place of **love**.

Is it possible to approach your body going forward with compassion and understanding? To make health choices with gentleness and care in mind instead of punishment? To do your movement/exercise from a sense of fun and respect instead of shame? To regard food and your appetites with curiosity and affirmation instead of chronic suspicion?

Consider whether your body, mind and spirit could benefit from this.

So what your body wants you to know today is:

There is no perfection outside of me for you to try to achieve. There is no perfection to strive for because we can't ever escape our foibles. We are already perfect in our wacky humanity. So we're gonna embrace the contradictions of who we are, wobbly bits and angular bits and all.

Bottom line: You actually don't need RULES for your food, your body, or your life. Once you develop true self-trust with all of this stuff, you can engage with it all with a genuine love and lightness that ACTUALLY serves you.

Much love,
Your body

Day 30

WHICH SIDE ARE YOU ON?

Hello, Darling,

When it comes to body stuff, there are two teams that you can choose to be on.

The first team is the team most of us were either forced onto via parental/medical authorities or drifted onto ourselves because of cultural conditioning.

This is the team of body hatred | chronic dieting | shame | body dissatisfaction | disordered eating | poor body image | food obsession | distrust in self.

It SUCKS being on this team, even though we're told it's the best team to be on. If we stay on this team, we're supposed to eventually get rewarded with good stuff like people liking us and accepting us and respecting us. We're supposed to end up liking ourselves, too, if we stay on this team long enough.

But there's actually another team that doesn't have nearly as much power or volume as the first team. It doesn't get sponsored by all the multinational corporations. And it has no marketing budget to speak of.

This is Team YOUR BODY.

Being on this team means sticking up for yourself and your body no matter what. It means setting boundaries that signal to yourself that you can trust yourself. Whether you're being body-shamed by a coworker or having your food policed by a family member, you are never apologetic, never ashamed; you're clearly and calmly on your body's side.

And when the call is coming from inside the house? Telling yourself you're not "allowed" to wear that thing because it's not "flattering?" You take that as the opportunity it is: to unlearn the patriarchal training that taught you "flattering" was a requirement for your life in the first place.

It's pretty tough to get on #TeamYourBody because once you've been recruited to the food-and-weight-obsession team, it's really hard to tear yourself away. Once that team gets lodged in your brain, then, HOO BOY, it feels like what they have to say is just THE TRUTH, plain and simple.

But what happens for folks is that they get tired. There are so many REQUIREMENTS of being on the body-obsession team. You always gotta be policing your food and monitoring your body and saying mean shit to yourself. You gotta be questioning yourself and doubting your appetites. You're supposed to despair if your clothes have a certain number sewn inside. It's just a huge mental and physical drain. So people start to wonder if there's a different way of relating to the body that isn't so replete with suffering.

When people stumble across this once-unfathomable idea that they could form an alliance with the enemy — i.e., their body — they may feel a combination of excitement and fear. It's scary to switch sides, for lots of reasons. There are fears about health, about what others will think, about the uncertainty and unfamiliarity of it all. There is so much to unlearn and relearn, and a whole new paradigm of the self to explore.

When you show up to be on #TeamYourBody, you don't accept bullshit from the diet and wellness industry anymore. You don't accept the idea that there's something wrong with you just for existing, or that you don't have the right to exist in the body that you inhabit today.

And contrary to what you may think, loving your body is NOT a prerequisite for being on #TeamYourBody (even though falling in love with your body can be a consequence of deciding to switch teams).

When it comes to body stuff, there are two teams that you can be on. You can be on the side of shame and fight your body, or you can choose your body's side and fight against shame.

Which side are you on?

Today, your body says,

When you choose to be on my side, there's something inside of me that just eases out. I feel so relaxed knowing that you've got my back. Knowing that we're working together feels like anything is possible. It feels like making genuinely good choices that are truly in our best interest. It feels like courage. It feels amazing.

Love,
Your Body

Day 31

A LOVE LETTER FROM THE AUTHOR

Hello, dearest Reader,

Well, we're at the finish line for this series of love letters. I hope you enjoyed reading them as much as I enjoyed writing them.

I have a few last thoughts for you.

We are chronically pelted with messages about the ways we should manipulate our bodies, so it's no wonder that we spend so much time thinking about how to manipulate our bodies.

The "you need to lose weight/change your body" chorus is extremely well-established in most people's minds.

Every time we hear those messages, they reinforce the well-grooved pathway in our minds where we hold it.

What very few of us have is the alternative message, just as firmly lodged in our brains.

What this means is that if you have a habit — perhaps cultivated over years or decades — of telling yourself that your body is wrong, bad, or broken, it's going to take a while to break that habit.

This is especially the case if you are one of the LEGIONS of people who either

a) had a mom who took you to Weight Watchers when you were nine or ten years old, and/or

b) had a pediatrician tell your parent that your developing-child-body was unacceptable, according to the BMI (a chart which is 100% pure, unadulterated bullshit).

If you've been telling yourself mean things for years, you definitely won't have stopped doing it in the mere 30 days you have been reading these daily love letters.

But I do hope that there is a tiny spot in your brain now that is receptive to the notion that perhaps your body isn't an abomination upon the world.

I like to focus on cultivating that little corner of my and other people's brains. It's in that corner where I write the counter-narratives to the ones we've heard all our lives (and that we still hear on a daily basis). I do this because I don't believe that body shame ever serves us. And we need a vast ocean of counter-narratives about the validity of our bodies to begin to counteract the lifetime of messages we've learned about how wrong they are.

If you want a slice of these counter-narratives, come sign up for my newsletter, *Bodytalk*, at bodytalk.substack.com

When you sign up, you'll automatically get a fresh love letter from your body, delivered every Thursday.

And if you decide you want to be a defector away from body shame and decamp to #TeamYourBody, I can teach you how. I'm a certified diet recovery coach who specializes in precisely that.

If you have thoughts, ideas, or questions about these love letters or anything I've written in them, I'd love to hear from you! Send me a message using the contact form on my website: schoolofbitchcraft.com/contact/

Remember: you are awesome, your body is a mind-blowing vessel of vibrant goodness, and there's nothing you need to do to change it.

Love,
Sabina (+ Your Body!)

www.ingramcontent.com/pod-product-compliance
Lightning Source LLC
Chambersburg PA
CBHW070334120526
44590CB00017B/2881